# MATRIX VISIONS

## HARRY WHITEWOLF

The parts may sound crazy, but somewhere
there's a whole that makes some kind of sense.

# MATRIX VISIONS

Curious verse containing given spiritual visions,
new findings, old tales and subjective interpretations.

Original of the above image: **The Giza Pyramids**
by Morhaf Kamal Aljanee (Own work) [CC BY-SA 3.0
(http://creativecommons.org/licenses/by-sa/3.0)],
licensed via Wikimedia Commons.

(Altered by mirroring, grayscale, cropping
by Harry Whitewolf.)

At the beginning of 2014, I went through what I can only describe as a 'spiritual epiphany regarding dark matters' (others may well call it a step away from insanity), where I was overloaded with 'downloaded' information that I tried to make sense of. This was up there in 'David Icke proportions' in how much it affected me, and I still find it hard to explain to other people the things I claim to know. One day I will write a book that is more straight talking, but for now, my insights have forced themselves out in the shape of this book of verse. Make of it what you will.

Thanks for reading,

Harry.

"The point appeared in the circle, yet wasn't.
Rather, it was the circle, traversed by the point.
To one who has completed the circle,
the point exists on the circumference.
The whole world I said is His imagination,
then I saw: His imagination is Himself."

- Shah Ni'matuallah.

***

"We shall roll up the heavens like a scroll rolled up for
books, as We began the first creation, We shall repeat it,
(it is) a promise binding upon Us. Truly, We shall do it."

- The Quran, chapter Al-Anbiya (21), verse number 104.

***

O Rose thou art sick.
The invisible worm,
That flies in the night
In the howling storm:
Has found out thy bed
Of crimson joy:
And his dark secret love
Does thy life destroy.

- The Sick Rose, William Blake.

"…Indian Mason was a… mighty man…
Raised up his little hand,
Said… I'm the little red snake...
A little red snake...
I've seen what he can do...making and making more of
God's children..."

-      Red Snake (song lyrics), Charles Manson.

\* \*\*

"It writhes! – it writhes! – with mortal pangs
The mimes become its food,
And seraphs sob at vermin fangs
In human gore imbued."

-      The Conqueror Worm, Edgar Allan Poe.

\*\*\*

"Man is the picture painted upon external matter, and
external matter is the individuality that surveys the
picture. "

-      The Rosicrucians: Their Rites and Mysteries (Third Edition),
Hargrave Jennings.

# CONTENTS

# THE MALICIOUS MAGICIANS

Welcome to the magic trick.

Welcome to the show.

Smoke and mirror tactics

Are truer than you know.

Welcome to the matrix,

Whose magic's only science.

Welcome to illusion

To which we've no defiance.


This is the conjurer's palace.

The home of malicious magicians;

Alien demons in smoky mirrors

Holding highest positions,

Whilst we're caught in the bottom

Of the great pyramid scheme,

Not giving a flying fuck but

Still living Puck's daydream.

Midsomer is fixed
Back into position,
Once a year at the Grove
In ritual vision.
The optic illusions
That we all know
Are everywhere.
That's truth to know.
Like that picture of
The girl and old hag.
One will see first,
Another, the last.
Like two profile faces
Forming a glass.
An old way of seeing
From forgotten pasts.
Like ancient shadows
Cast by solstice spots.
That is the truth
That we forgot.

Like the ancients seeing
The bull in the sky,
Instead of stars,
'Cos they were a lie.

There began the magic trick.
Gradual plans aren't noticed.
We didn't see our eyes devolve
Over the time cast by our hostess.

The magic trick
Has always been.
That is why
It can't be seen.

The malicious magicians
Are running this matrix.
Hypnotised us from the start
With dodgy damn magi tricks.

We're in the red snake matrix,
Please make no mistake.
We're in bed with the serpent
Of everything that's fake.
All is smoke and mirrors.
All is an illusion.
All is God imprisoned,
Awaiting absolution.
The malicious magicians
Began this damn show.
The great entertainment
That we'd never know
We were a part of,
'Cos we cannot see
Beyond our own
Personalities.

This is the snake matrix,
With all of its fake tricks
And all of its hate kicks,
God, it makes me sick,
So let's not take the stick.

To action, let's go. Quick.
Knock down all the bricks
And all false politics.
Stop getting our fix
With T.V channel mix,
Because we're being dicks.
Get out of this matrix.
See the smoke and mirror tricks.
Get out of the snake matrix.

Welcome to the magic trick.
Welcome to the show.
Smoke and fairground mirrors
Are truer than you know.

# STRANGE LANDS

I've been to the strange lands

of alien wastelands.

I've seen red snakes writhe

and still got out alive.

I've been to the bad lands;

seen ancient battle plans.

I've been to the mad lands

that few can understand.

I've bathed in the hate lands,

played with crooked straight hands,

far away from mainlands

of reality's chain lands.

I've not strayed from good,

because I never would,

but I've seen the wastelands

of alien strange lands.

They're here where we all stand.

The demonic hate lands.

The alien wastelands.

I've been to the strange lands.

# WRONG DOORS

Doors should never open
to the same place twice.
If they do, then it's you
who will pay the price.
It's walls and roads
that make the maze.
Cities are labyrinths;
the causes of craze.

The animals laugh
at our weak skin
And this detachment
that we are in.
Suckling on Satan's
teat of milk sin.
No human kindness
left in our kin.

Windows should be opened
beyond an arm's reach.
Pick up the horizon's
line on the beach.
Parallel lines cross
out there somewhere.
Perspective is the lost
cross we all bear.

We're herded with burdens
over cattle grids,
Making unkind capitalist
damn banker bids.
Doors should never open
to the same place.
If they do, then you
are caught in the maze.
This laboratory
labyrinth craze.
This absurd Word of
godly dis-grace.

Taste the metallic
sound of the maya.
Find a whore and ignore
her or just pay her.
Hear the flavour that's beyond
the kindergarten science.
Without the plug we cannot
study the appliance.
If you see the truth,
you may have defiance,
but know your place amongst
the secret alliance.

Doors should never open
to the same place twice or more.
If they do, then you've lost your way,
so try another door.

# THE OWL

The time turned to twenty two,

And by my window, an owl flew.

In fact, the owl came right through,

The glass, with a t-wit-t-woo.

Saying, "Hello, how do you do?

I am Elohim. My name YAH-WOOH."

"Hello owl," I said in return.

"Have you wisdom for me to learn?"

"Of course," said he. "That much is true,

But don't think me a Swift Yahoo."

"Of course not," I said to the bird.

"Good," said he, "I hate that word."

There was a pause, and then he said,

"I wonder, would you like my head?"

And with that, my vision did change.

My eyes were sideways; rearranged.

And I looked upon this brand new world,

Which the owl had uncurled,

From the upward downward spiral,

With a golden love filled smile.

"This is the world the gods do see,"

Said the wise owl unto me.

"I thank you indeed," I said to him,

"Dear YAH-WOOH of Elohim,

For showing me such a sight as this.

Why there's so much a man can miss!"

"Indeed," he replied and my head returned,

And 'twas hard to remember what I'd learnt.

I looked at the owl, that old bird wise.

I said, "Oh damn these bloody eyes!"

But he condemned me and said, "Don't judge.

Be grateful, for you've seen the smudge,

That many men won't dare believe,

'Cos two eyes only always deceive."

At my quick temper, I was ashamed,

But he forgave and gave no blame.

Then the owl's head turned into gold,

And the air in the room did turn cold,

As the number three flew from his brow,

And his round head opened to allow,

12

The golden light to ebb and flow,

'Til it settled above as below,

And changed into a sinful fruit.

A golden apple of Absolute.

The old wise owl had quite vanished.

Leaving only the apple banished.

So I picked it up, and it turned deep red,

And I saw the world through that other head.

I bit into the apple filled with sin,

Then I tasted the blood of my own skin,

And I went to bed, feeling anew,

Whistling to myself, "T-wit, t-woo."

# DOLLAR BILL DEVILS AND DOGS

Debate the All Seeing Eyed pyramid

On a damn dollar bill, all day.

An example of distraction tricks

That society always displays.

Talk about the object,

When the truth can be found,

By looking at the blurs,

In the hard to see background.

Back of a 2007 **U.S. one-dollar bill**. (Public Domain.)
(Detail. Pyramid removed.)

14

In political spin and images both,

The same tactics are at play.

So let us look at the creatures

On the damn dollar bill's display.

 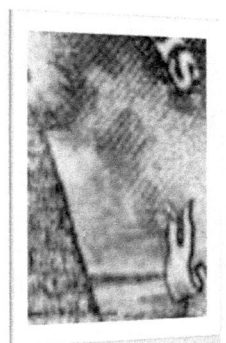

You can locate a Grey alien,

If you view it from one perspective,

But like seeing a young girl or old hag,

The optic illusion is multi-effective.

For the head of the alien

Is also an ear

Of a cartoon dog head,

If you let it appear.

But the alien head-dog ear

Is also but a snout

Of the beast above.

And do not miss out,

On it also being the nose

Of the large frowning clown face.

Then look around a little more,

In the dollar bill matrix maze;

Like turning that alien clown

Around to see another dog.

But nothing can be proven, 'cos

Pictures are hidden in fog.

Try mirroring the dollar bill pic,
And you will see plenty more.
But you've always got to look around,
If you really want to explore;
'Cos there are many ways of seeing
These New World Order totem poles,
Containing dogs, devils, spiders, owls,
From the wides, to the bigs to the smalls.

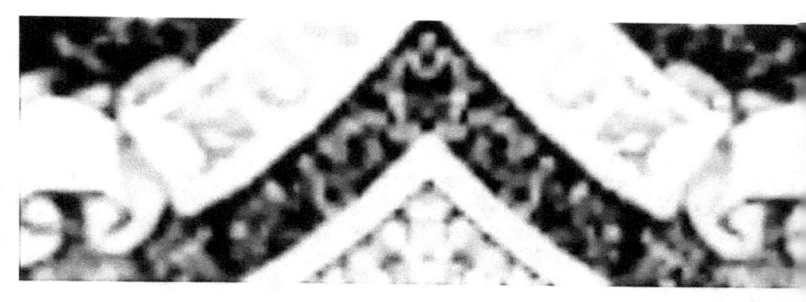

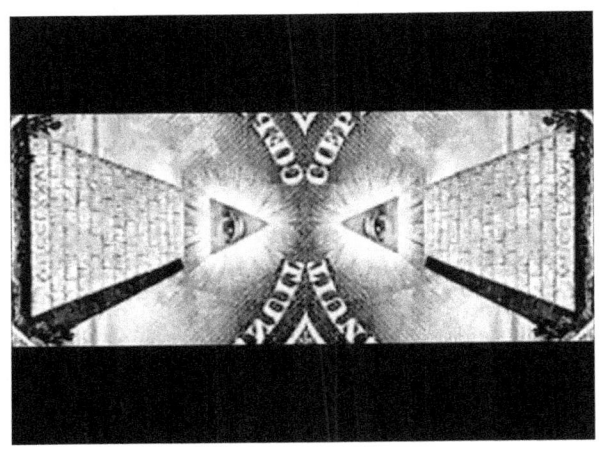

19

Then take it a crazy step further.

Change polar opposites with Photoshop.

There you will find a cartoon imp,

With a scythe; ready to chop,

As he hangs over the sign

Stating objectives.

Order for the New Age.

Or is this all subjective?

# NUMERICAL RAIN

Three is the magic number

Of sideways McDonald's M.

Seen Lloyd's bank's black horse logo?

You'd better look again,

For if you look you may see

The twos which are encrypted.

In the Queen's eye on a note,

You'll also see them scripted.

And in the running number rain

That's always there 'tween space.

It's easy to see the matrix,

If you look in the right place.

Background buzz is raining down.

Bookshelves shiver with stories.

Find the cracks running real

And you will find God's glories.

Past the deceiving evil eyes.

Past the digital numbers.

Run back to the Love of Source

And forget all earthly hungers.

All of the numbers raining down,

Running scripts, just like the movie.

Only it's not green that is the code.

Red's the disguise that's truly

The matrix raining down around

Us, yet we're also it.

Darkness is where love is,

'Cos everything's opposite.

Darkness is where truth was

Before this world was lit.

We are all just numbers

And yet we don't get it.

# RED SNAKE RULES

The Red Snake rules.

The Red Snake winds.

Make no mistake,

He drinks our wines.

Sacrament

For the serpentine.

Drinking blood,

The serpent winds.

With piercing fangs,

And origins,

Of vampires' vague

Beginnings.


Sinning serpent spread your fear.

Turn and twist and disappear.

Winding snake take a side walk,

In Jesus and Mary's chain of talk.

Stalker serpents invading minds.
Watch the phallus grow and grind.


Deep Red Snake
Who hypnotises.
Creeping worms
Bury surprises.


Deep in the sockets of eyes and
All the pockets of flesh's island.
Take a sigh and return to the snake
Who twists and turns in hellish mistakes,
Feeding on our wine just for the take,
Writhing around our souls with a quake.
The serpent of danger. The dragon of anger.
The twisting turning winding two fanger.
Vampires were here before their fake stories.
Wind with the Red Snake and you'll see its glories.
Gone are the secrets and yet they're still there.
Just look at the blood moon and start running scared.

The Red Snake is winding.

The Red Snake is turning.

The serpent is spinning.

The Devil is learning.

Make no mistake,

The Red Snake winds.

He turns and twists

And drinks our wines.

# THE TORTURE OF CREATION

Spirit was broken

and unspoken things

came to pass

in misery's stings.

Hard was the touch.

Brittle were bones.

Twisting ether to flesh

amongst tortured moans.

In mysteries' songs

we'll remember the pain.

Never would we choose

the same fate again.

Born into bondage

of broken bones.

Death is forever

in our new homes.

Exploding in material
not before known.
Bursting in stench taste,
forgetting our thrones.

Any godly kingdom
once known was quickly banished.
We are sadomasochists,
and we chose to be punished.

# HOW TO GET A FACE IN ADVERTISING

If you have worked in sales, you'll know:
If you smile, your customer will too.
That's why back in the old days (fact:)
Clock faces in ads would show ten to two-
A well-known tactic still used sometimes.
Clock hands making a smile.
See a smile and you'll smile back
And buy the product all the while.

So why has nobody noticed
The present day everywhere grin
Used in most every logo and
Every bit of advertising?
Amazon, Argos, ao.
National Lottery. Nike. LG.
IHOP. Danone. Kraft Foods.
TUI Group. Coca Cola. Pepsi.

And so many smiles on the net.
Subliminal smiles are everywhere.
Smile back and buy the product,
'Cos they're all grinning with a stare.

And there will always be letters,
To give the suggestion of eyes,
So let's put the oo into Google
And Yahoo! and see the eye-spies.

See the devil's tail too, in Amazon's smile,
And whilst we're at it, you might as while
Turn Google's **g** logo, upon its side.
The glasses are watching. We're being con spied.

The clock face set at ten to two,
Was only the first trick that they knew.
And yet even that smile ain't quite true,
'Cos if you want to see my madness through,

You'll see the smile made by clock hands,
Is nothing of the sort.
They are frowning eyes and devil horns,
Used to suppress our every thought.

# THE GREEN MAN'S FACE

I have seen the Green Man's face.

I've heard his voice upon the wind.

I've seen him hiding in the trees,

Dancing with satyrs of sin.

I've seen him stare straight at me.

I've seen his face change into many.

I have seen green skulls speak darkness

Into rotten ears they leant me.


The trees themselves are wise and good,

But legion they do become.

Branches bear Satan face origins

And all that he has done.


Look like you're looking at a painting,

For that is all it is.

A film reel of snapshots of mugshots.

We are the cameras, this

Is our movie.

Take front row seats.

But the twat with the big hat

Ain't being discrete.

So it's back to the trees;

Camouflaged pictures.

In leaves and angles

We'll find old scriptures.

Through branches and twigs,

We'll greet the Green Man

And all in his likeness,

As part of the plan.

Through trunks and skies,

Green Man will be met.

Piper Pan; two horned,

Who's names they have stretched

Into so many,

Both good and bad.

But this is his source

That I'm hinting at.

The Green Man's face,

I've seen it.

The Green Man's face,

I've been it.

Look again,

With alien eyes.

Pretend you're an owl

And look at the skies,

Between the branches,

Where you'll see the faces,

If you learn how to see

Negative spaces.

If you learn how to see

Like American clans

Where shadows were pictures

Stretched out on the land.

Showing the two halves

Of the infinite coin.

They used to see

All the stars as points.

Great bears and bulls

Clustered the sky

When they were looked at

With an ancient eye.

Dot to dot did

Begin back then.

That and so many

Other inventions,

But now's not the time

To mention them.

So it's back to Green Man

And the author of men.

The battle of gods

In a red painted den.

We're words on a parchment

From some great bard's pen.


We are a carousel

Going round and round.

If we stopped, the simple

Truth would soon be found.

We'd see through the slits,

Those one one ones,

Those prison bars

For whom we've spun,

And view the truth

On the other side

Of this hypnosis

Life of lies we've lied.


The eyes are awaiting,

Away from the carousel.

I can see them clearly,

And I can see their spell.


Absurdity is truth, if

You wanna know how it is.

Dali melted time because

He was a hypnotist,

Who could walk into pictures,

Like ancients of old,

Only they saw the images

Out there in the cold,

Between the branches,
In negative spaces,
They saw Satan's army
And all of their faces.

I've seen the Green Man;
Hijacked by the bad.
And we're cutting down trees.
Damn, that makes me so sad.
Know the truth.
Look to the trees
And the beyond,
And hear the breeze.
See the world
How it really is;
A spinning carousel
Of hellish bliss

Being played out

For stupid damn games.

I've seen the Green Man

And I know his names.

# NUMBER SECRETS

The pyramid

is a cross from above.

The heart symbol

does not depict love.

The first is two ones.

The second two twos.

Threes form an eight

of an eternal noose.

Eight is the hourglass

taking our hours;

Though it's easily turned

by those in power.

Three sixes are three eyes;

the two and the one,

Seen on their side;

a Horus Thoth sum.

38

Three eyes watching
us from the dark.
Six six six,
that beastly mark.
Christ is number four
but he wears Satan's face.
Seven's a semi-pyramid
and zero is misplaced.
Two ones are two,
but they're still two ones.
Snake eyes are three.
Let's redo our sums.

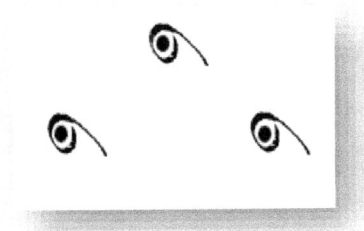

# THE MONSTER

As I arrived home one wicked night,

I encountered a most insipid sight,

For 'twas not at all to my flavour,

Let alone to my kind favour,

That I saw the horrid sight;

A monster of such fiendish fright,

Sent to me upon that night.

The creature looked at me with spite.

And if I might describe the monster to you,

It was much like this, within my view:

The creature had a building's face

With eyes of needles much misplaced

And the nose of a toy aeroplane

And lips of spouts. The face was plain.

Well, I was frightened and more than forlorn,

At this creature with ears of yellow sweetcorn.

His shoe tongue stuck out and then his

Cave mouth blew me a little kiss

And I espied the creature's broken comb teeth,

And I must admit, I could scarcely believe

What I was seeing. But there he stood.

A giant monster up to no good.

I tried to take in his huge pin head,

Then looked him up and down instead.

He had a bottle neck. He had clock hands,

Upon settee arms that were so grand.

He had table feet upon legs of chairs.

Then once more in his needle eyes I stared,

And that's when he vanished. In a blink.

Leaving me with many things to think.

Then I went inside my little house,

And I began to laugh at myself,

For it was soon clear that the creature so strange

Was no more than my house rearranged.

# THE DOOR TO REALITY

Perceive the world through two lenses.

Try to make sense with five senses.

We think that colour's really there,

In the sky or in that chair.

What we see is upside down.

It's our brains that wear that frown.

What we think is solid form,

Is energy. That is the norm.

Everything we think we know.

Is just a shadowed magic show.

We think we're top of the food chain,

When we are nosh for gods insane.

Believing everything we see,

Because we do instead of be.

They laugh at us, 'cos we're the fool.

Barely out of primordial school.

They keep us locked within a bubble.

In a world of constant trouble.

Believing things they know are double.

Like photographs taken from Hubble.

Photoshopped with alien ease.

Pictures of Mars could just be Greece.

How do we know what we see,

Is in fact reality,

If the world is governed by,

The Alien Seeing Eye?

I don't believe a thing I see.

Sometimes an elf can be a tree.

Sometimes a witch can be a cat.

From the right angle, the world is flat.

From the right perspective, space can stop,

Into a Truman Show backdrop,

Where there's a door to reality.

That's the world that I do see.

# THE STRAIGHT AND NARROW

A straight line is only part of a curve,

Bent by those to whom we serve.

If I had the nerve I'd tell you the truth,

But I have nothing in the way of proof.

We look like cross eyed fools to them,

When that fool is actually wiser than men.

Roll out the carpet and stick out your tongue.

Red is the colour that we have become.

Riding down highways way past heaven.

We are, all of us, aliens' brethren;

Microscopic all important ants.

But if we could only pause a glance,

You'd see the truth I allude to.

One hand claps when there aren't two,

But do two hands make the sound of clapping?

Or is it the sound of the mirror cracking?

Trapping us in the image of God.

Shaking our heads in the world of nod.

Look again and you will see

We're only crabs in a harsh sea.

Thinking we're big fish when the pond's so small.

What would the world look like if we were tall?

As tall as trees reaching to the moon.

We are just shadows cast at noon.

On the straight and narrow of the thin line.

We are bent backwards to way behind time.

# THE GREAT CARTOON

See the parts but not the whole.

Spot the ball but miss the goal.

Humans do not see with soul.


Broaden your perspective,

And see like the selective,

'Cos objects are subjective.


Two houses hundreds of miles apart

Could be two eyes if not seen in part.

Welcome to snake matrix art.


Where is the face then? Climb to the moon.

Then look back down with alien zoom

And you will see the great cartoon.

# THE PENTAGON'S HIDDEN HALF

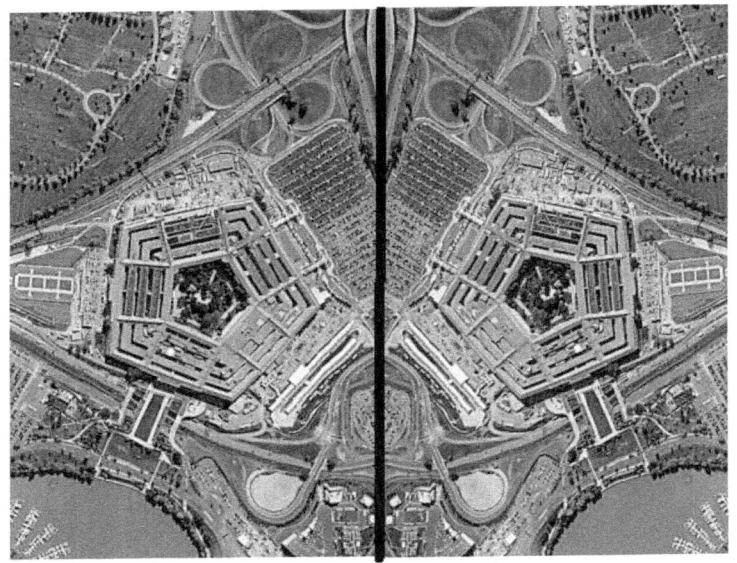

**The Pentagon** (April 2002). Source: World Wind. Author: NASA.
Licensed under Public Domain via Wikimedia Commons.
**(Mirrored.)**

The Pentagon, U.S.A.

Not only Satanic in name.

Mirror the half to see the whole.

The faces should be plain.

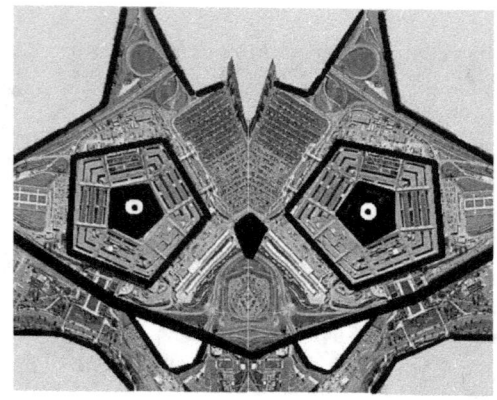

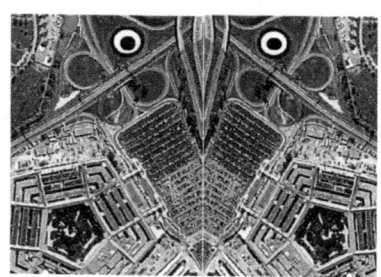

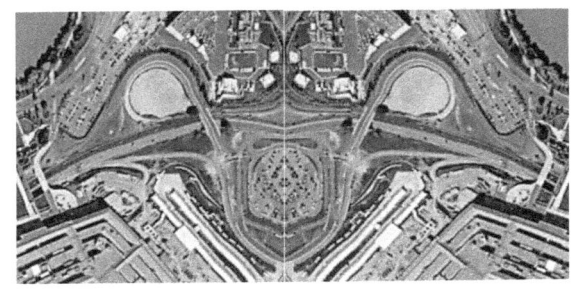

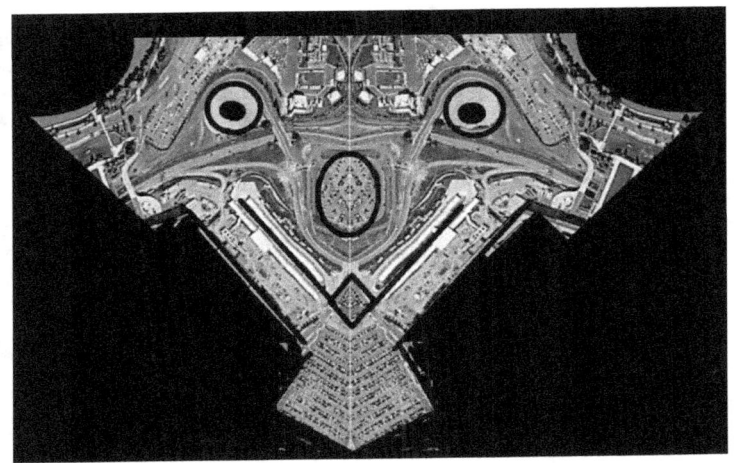

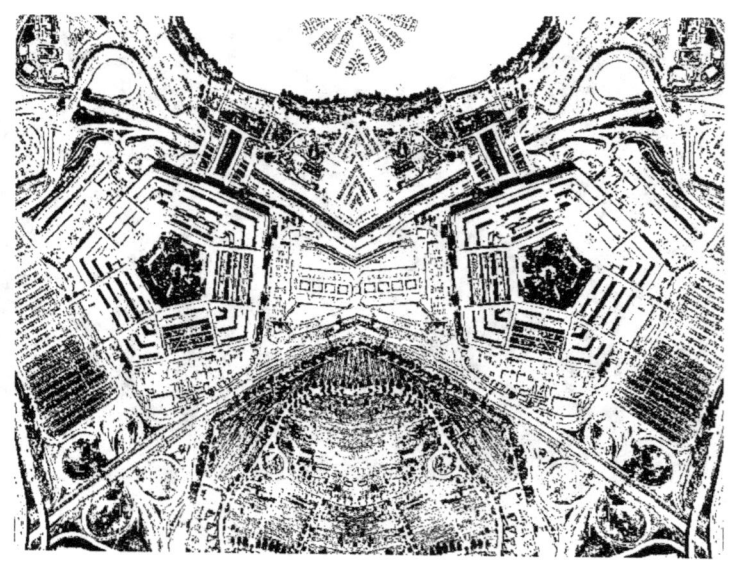

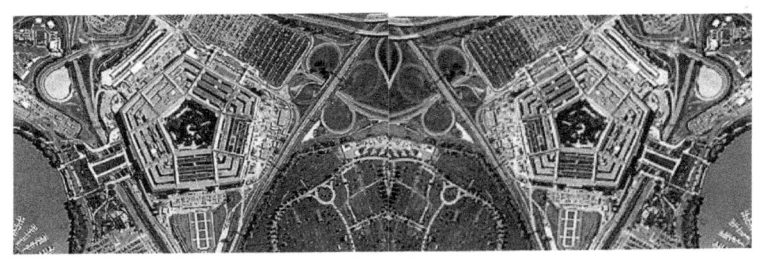

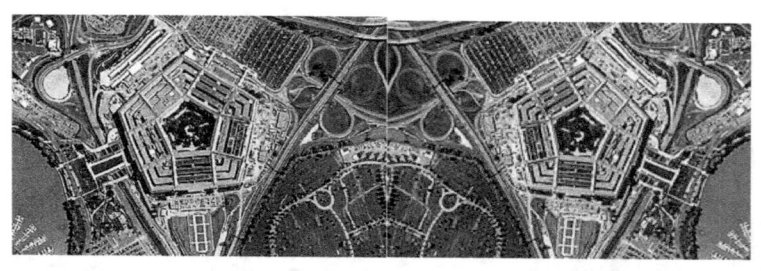

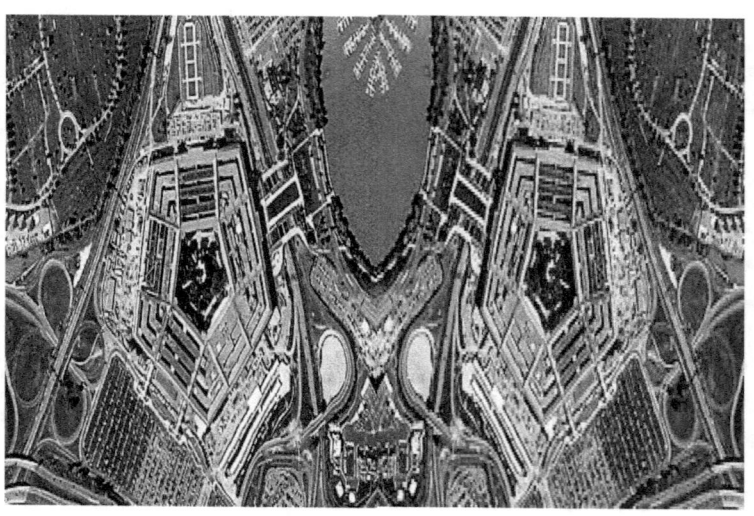

(Stretched.)

52

(Lightened/stretched.)

53

(Stretched.)

54

(Stretched.)

55

# THE OLD NEW CREATURES

I'm a creature of habit

And a habit of creature.

Find your own truth.

I'm just my own teacher.

I do not ask you

For anything.

Not that you believe

My silly ramblings.

This is just my truth.

I wish it were not,

But I'm a good penny

That won't fit the slot.

I am light and darkness,

And all that is.

I'm the absurdity

Of Satan's kiss.

We are not lords.

We are not preachers.

We are just habits

Of the new creatures.

# SATAN'S SPINNING TOP

When the Earth stops spinning

We will know God.

That was the first trick

The Devil did prod;

Spinning the Earth

Like a spinning top.

Round and round we go.

If we could stop

The spinning carousel,

We would see,

That we've been in Hell

And the

Truth would be found

In fractals of God.

And fragments of devils

Would no longer prod.

# UNSWEETENED ROSE

Aliens. Demons.

What's in a name?

Creations of Man

are all the same.

# THE SERVANT OF PAN

A servant of Pan,

Flew up to a man,

And said, "Tell me what you know."

To which he replied,

"Why, I know that I've died,

A hundred times or so."

The servant of Pan,

Again asked the man,

"Tell me what you know. Please do."

The man said that he,

Knew of eternity

And that matter can be seen through.

The servant of Pan,

Then questioned the man,

With, "What do you know of this place?"

He said, "Numbers and names,

They are all the same.

Each one creates the same face."

The servant of Pan,

Was irked by the man.

He knew much more than he should.

The spell had been broken.

His words: plain and open.

The servant could take no more good.

He yelled at the man,

That servant of Pan,

And disappeared in a puff of smoke.

The man just smiled,

Relaxed all the while,

For everything was just a joke.

# DEAD MAN WALKING

I'm not on the make.

I'm William Blake.

I'm Depp's Dead Man,

if you understand.


By achieving selflessness,

I can become anyone,

my guardian angel

did tell me once.

I can be Blake

reincarnated

if I want to be.

If I was fated.

But first I must

be Nobody,

If you maybe know

the Jarmusch movie.

I am the Native
with one downfall fix;
Always trying to get
his tobacco sticks.
I am the Dead Man,
as we all are.
I am Blake driving
a beat up old car.
I'm Milton, I'm
Bunyan and you.
I'm Hilton, the
sun and the dew.
I am all that has been
and all that will be,
'cos I remember the
call given to me.
I can be Blake
in another dimension,
or a dream that Shakespeare
once did mention.

What's in a name?

That was the curse.

When naming took

place in its first.

The thirst of the poets

will always sup,

From the past

and present's cup,

But the future will

be made in visions.

Thought creates

our world's decisions.

Take your places

and envision good.

Ten minutes a day.

Know that you should.

Help the down trodden

and those in need.

Stop your damn

capitalist greed.

See what we

have thrown away.

All aspire

to selfless ways.


I'm William Blake.

I'm not on the make.

I'm a Depp Dead Man,

if you understand.

# AN ILLUMINATI PROVERB

In the land of two eyed men,

The three eyed man is king.

# HALO EYE

The halo over a head,

Seen from above is an eye.

Mexican frying an egg

Perspective tricks to fix the lie.


We see the faces.

They see the glass.

They see the present.

We see the past.

# THE SECRET SPHINX

Turn the Sphinx's head upside down,
And see the optical illusion.
Locate a new set of eyes
And you'll see a cat's protrusion,
As clear as mud when you see it,
Just like a magic eye picture.
Everything is double-more
In the hidden scripture.

Then look at the shadows
Cast by different angles
And you'll find the devils,
Dogs, and animals.

(Above image: eyes added.)

The Sphinx 977.PNG By Ijanderson977 (Own work) [Public domain], via Wikimedia Commons.

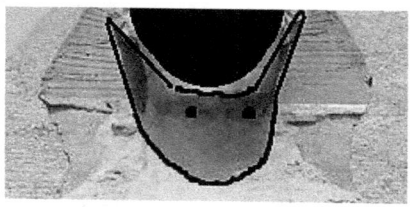

Mirror, mirror,

Mirror, mirror,

Might make things

A little clearer…

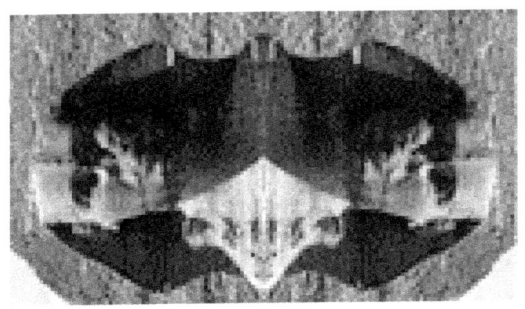

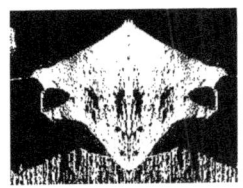

Sphinx und Chephren-Pyramide.jpg By Christian Rosenbaum. (Mirrored.)

# THE TRUTH IS CATS AND DOGS

Everything's backwards.

Can't you see?

Fake Devil did make

this world for we.

This world you are of.

Forge forwards do.

We are a mirror

split into two.

We feel like we're missing

another half,

because that's the truth

of life's drudge path.

We have been severed.

We have been blinded.

Cast into light;

by darkness we're binded.

Everything's backwards.

You worship false gods.

The truth may sound silly

but the true god is dog.

Praise the Black Dog

and the Holy Cat.

Life's a cartoon

(he says with no tact).

We're three dimensional,

but really we're two.

We are the bones

on which the dogs chew.

We were once one,

before we were flat.

Then we were two,

before dogs and cats

scrolled up the universe

in three dimensions.

There was the apple.

First bite to be taken.

Before we were bones

and pieces of meat,

we were seraphim,

in holy seats.

But with the temptation,

we took the first bite.

Cast into 3D

with all of its frights.

Death was made real;

what once was a myth.

Look for Fake Devil.

In this world he lives.


This is Red Matrix:

damn time and space tricks,

because the truth is

neither do exist.


We're split into two worlds,

in three, four dimensions.

We're really 2D.

Is that beyond comprehension?

74

We were once one.

Then we were two.

And we still are,

though we don't know it's true.


Everything is backwards.

This is death. It's not life.

Truth's so hard to handle,

when carrying the knife.

But cutting through the bullshit,

these words couldn't be plainer.

The truth is cats and dogs

are running this container.


We're here for entertainment.

We're damn rats in a cage.

Unscroll the universe;

see how cartoons are made.

We're nothing but fractals

made in our image.

The Fake Devil has us.

He's in our lineage.

He is our Father.

We've forgotten our first;

Before there was Eden,

when we were damn cursed.


When we stop

space and time,

then we'll see

the Devil's crime.


When we stop

time and space

then we'll see

the Devil's face.


Everything is backwards.

We're in the looking glass.

Forgotten our others.

Into Hell we're cast.

And we call it *life*.

And we're proud to be human.

We love our families

and we try to be true men,

but everything's backwards.

That's why they laugh.

We're in Hell right now.

Fell from the path.


The family's the Devil's children.

Humanity's his creation.

The Fake Devil has us by the balls

and he loves our celebrations.

But the Fake Devil is only

made up of dogs and cats.

And they are only two

dimensional toons at that.

Unscroll the world.

Unroll yourself.

Look through the eyes

of someone else.

An alien demon's
way of seeing.
Broaden perspectives.
Truth's for the freeing.

Stop time and space.
There, you'll find God.
Not the coward charlatan
played by cats and dogs,
but the true God forgotten.
The one dimension.
The source. The Love
beyond comprehension.

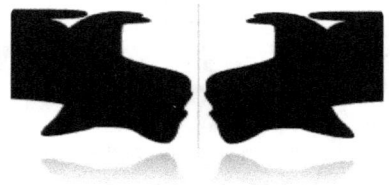

# THE 11:11

Seasons' time goes round in circles.

Age is the time that's straight.

The two together make a spiral,

Spinning round like a plate

On a stick, the zero and one.

The binary we have become

Since we strayed from Heaven's Gate.


The eleven eleven

Are all just ones.

Carousel slit bars

Are spun by cunts.

The eleven eleven,

The linear line.

The linear lie.

The very worst crime.

The eleven eleven

The cracks of God

Shining through

With angelic nods.

The eleven eleven

The number one.

No straight lines in nature.

We have become

Like the Roman curse,

And early cross,

Before it was lengthened

In Christian dross.

The eleven eleven

The truth's at the centre,

Where two swords cross

To make only one fencer.

The eleven eleven.

The binary half,

Along with the zero;

The circle of craft.

The cross in the circle.

Spin it around.

These are the tricks

To which we are bound.


Seasons' time goes round and round.

Timelines are always straight.

Together the two do spiral,

Spinning round fake fate.

Everything is zeroes and ones.

The binary code we have become

Since we strayed from Heaven's Gate.

# MADE IN GOD'S IMAGE

Why's God's image so important?

I wonder if he's vain.

Why is it that we look like him?

Can anyone explain?

Maybe we are only images.

That is the truth so plain.

Maybe we're just pictures

In an alien video game.

# SEEING WITH NON-HUMAN EYES

See how aliens see.

See the world's disguise.

Not through two looking fake forwards.

See through alien eyes.

Imagine your eyes are crossed mirrors.

View the world as a pixelated blur.

Imagine you have a dozen eyes

Where different sights will occur.

Imagine everything spherical,

'Cos no straight lines can be seen.

Imagine everything concave

Or split into a multi-screen.

Imagine you can see for miles.

Imagine you have x-ray eyes,

Infrared and ultraviolet sight,

And microscope sight to spy.

Focus is deception.

It happens to harden our touch.

There is no one behind us,

Because there is no such

Thing as direction

Or a fixed object.

Use quantum eyes

To see worlds reflect.

Look at the world

With alien eyes.

See its design,

And all of our lies.

# THE GOLDEN SPIRAL SECTION

The Golden Section.

Beauty's a lie.

It's the magic trick

That'll fix your eye.

Turning the spiral

In your own vision,

So that the illusion

Of space is given.

The Golden Section.

The door to beyond.

The mathematical code

On Golden Pond.

The Golden Section.

The crossing lines;

A spiral staircase

For us to climb.

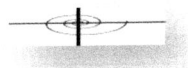

# IN FIRES

In fires, the pictures of old were seen.

Burning bright without the green.

Red and yellow. Orange and blue.

Better shows than BBC 2.

In the light, and through the smoke,

The ancient other beings spoke.

The mist would rise into the air,

Framing everything there;

In the unseen of the world around.

In the smoke, the truth was found.

In crystal balls; those mirror spheres,

Could be seen the mousetrapped years.

In the clouds, stories were told.

And in the trees were tales of old.

All pure waters reflected truth.

And all the stars did shine with youth.

Faces in mountains and spaces framed.

This was the world before 'twas named.

Seeing the truth in a heatwave blur.

Slowing our speed, for truth to occur.

Pausing ourselves to see life as it is.

These are the pictures that we all miss.

We've consolidated all those blurs and reflections,

In a hard light reality of false perceptions.

See the world once again like stories of old.

Don't fear to admit that we've been cajoled.

See who you are in a simple glass pane.

Don't look at the world in the same way again.

# ELECTRIC LIZARDS

Remember before the dark lightning storm,

When electric lizards came to keep us warm.

Remember the promises that were once sworn,

When spirit bodies were stretched and torn.

Remember be wary, 'cause we have been warned.

Remember ere we were elemental born.

Beware of dark metals that create each new dawn.

Remember before the dark lightning storm.

## STOP

Quicker and quicker and faster and faster.

We walk in time with our unknown master.

Striding forwards, faster and quicker.

The slowness of truth is now but a flicker.

## ANIMAL THINKING

Did we think in words before there were words?

Without words, what did thoughts sound like?
Did the Word invade the peacefulness of our minds?
The great Logos of the psych.

# THE EARTH IS FLAT

The Earth is flat.

It was scrolled round.

We think we're clever,

But we've been bound

To lies for so long,

That now we forget,

The universe is flat.

That is the secret.

# DOG COLLAR

Give society's man the coded dress.

Hang his neck in a Mason noose tie.

Lead him by the leash he's knotted himself,

Like the dog he is in the lie.

See his collar. Those two dog ears;

Upside down, pointed horns.

Watch him in his ancient bear skin,

Whose carcass flesh is torn.

Thinking we're the model modern human.

Oh if only we were so bold.

No, we're just still trying to survive

Inside away from the cold.

Dress us up any way you please.

Lead us like dogs on leashes,

Just like we dress up our poodles.

Simply because it pleases.

Dress up the dogs

And give them cigars

In society's snare

Of drunken bars.

We are the dogs

Eating dogs eating

Dogs eating hot dogs

With dressing and seas'ning.

Dress up the poodles.

We're laptop lapdogs.

Tied in money nooses;

Wannabe prince frogs.

Give society's man the coded dress.

Hang his neck in a Mason noose tie.

Lead him by the leash he's knotted himself,

Like the dog he is in the lie.

# FIBONACCI'S FIB

Fibonacci's sequence

causes left brain thinking.

Water spiralling in us

is not fit for drinking.

Blindfold us

and we will spiral

into oceans'

moon pulled tidal.

Left or right

in the hemispheres.

Let's turn right

and shed our tears.

Become the ocean

that they've spun.

Remember that

we are all one.

See before Adam
and his rib.
Fibonacci.
The great fib.

# FLESH MACHINES

Humanity. Humanity.

Invented for insanity.

Humanity. Humanity.

Made for Satan's vanity.

What a damned calamity.

We're so proud of humanity.


Try to remember before we were bones.

When we could see without eyes.

Remember how we used to view,

Before we were built upon lies.

They gave lenses to deceive us,

And know the purpose of touch,

Was to separate the oneness

Into single objects and such.

Our brains are alien microchips

Implanted in the soul.

They trapped God in flesh machines

And played with us like dolls.

We're pets and snacks.
We're children of sin.
But that's only the matter
That we're contained in.
So it doesn't matter,
Because inside and out,
We are still oneness.
Of that I've no doubt.

Flesh machines will fry one day.
Fresh spirits will take the place
Of the fake gaol we're cast into.
Be a new human race.
One that's connected
With everything.
Remembering when
We were all seraphim.

A new birth is waiting.
We are in labour.
Brothers and sisters,
Mothers and neighbours,

Find the truth

That you've forgotten.

Taste fresh fruit.

Forget the rotten.

Humanity. Humanity.

Invented for insanity.

What a damned calamity.

We're so proud of humanity.

# THE QR CODE CODE

QR codes are magic eye pictures.

Un-pixelate and blur.

View them in the right way

And you'll see faces occur.

Animals and demons

With simple cartoon smiles.

Scan the QR codes,

Which are merely fractal tiles

Of the larger image.

The parts make a whole,

Because everything is

Under control.


But QR codes are no big deal.

Just a hint of the matrix mazes.

Go on, stare at the encoded

And see the hidden faces.

Don't scan the QR code
But stop and stare,
'Cos you'll find a magic
Eye picture there.

Though the clever thing
About the QR code is
There's so much to see
And so much to miss.

By Maly LOLek (Own work) [Public domain], via Wikimedia Commons

By ORCID, Inc. [Public domain], via Wikimedia Commons

By Mxs02 (Own work) [CC BY-SA 4.0
(http://creativecommons.org/licenses/by-sa/4.0)], via Wikimedia Commons

# KNOWING THE APPLE

From the pip, the apple grew.

Knowledge would become anew.

From the seed the tree would grow.

New made fruit to sense and know.

Not just taste, but touch as well,

Came from that first apple's spell.

Turned from gold and painted red.

The apples planted in our heads.

The trees have grown with many branches.

With new choices came new chances.

Now we've forgotten Snow White's tale.

We are the apple. This is Hell.

The heart is the apple viewed in 2D,

And the 3 is on top of the devil V.

3 is the m and the w.

Pyramid ram heads for all to view.

Man and Woman and God, the three.

The Fake Devil's Holy Trinity.

V is the horns and half of the X
Which marks the spot of aerial secrets.
V is the five with the three and two.
Fibonacci's pattern is a good clue.
So all that's needed are two hiding ones,
Which did not even exist once,
Before the apple was offered for taste,
Which we took in good faith and haste.
From the pip, the red apple grew,
And yet we think our planet's blue.
The golden apple's painted red.
Its seeds have scattered and they've spread.
The rotten apple's no longer gold.
Here's life: the great lie that they sold.
Take a bite of the apple red.
Believe the dream inside your head.

# FREAK SHOW PEEPSHOWS

We are filthy freaky freak show peepshows,

Eating burritos bitten by mosquitoes,

Wishing that we were all Beatles

Instead of freaky people viewed through peepholes.

Discover devil horns in all the steeples.

We are just the freaky toy town people.

Then go even further down that dark deep hole,

And see liars have hooked us on bloody spiked meat poles.

# ALIEN ACUPUNCTURE

Knock down Cleopatra's Needle

And all the global obelisks.

They are all damn routers of

Alien acupuncturists.

Precisely placed to stab ley lines,

And divert the veins of Earth.

Pinning us down in hypnosis,

Since our first day of birth.

Knock down the demon needles that

Keep us stuck at this juncture.

Bring back the map of Mother Nature,

Not that of alien acupuncture.

# PERSPECTIVE'S TEASE

A camel can pass through a needle's eye,

But still the rich can't enter heaven.

A stitch in time did sew the crime

Perpetrated by demon brethren.

A needle in a haystack

Is so easy to find,

If you have a magnet

Of the largest kind.

Can't see the forest

For the trees;

Those one one trunks

Of perspective's tease.

# THE ALL SEEING EYES

The All Seeing Eye

Ain't up in the sky

Or atop a pyramid

Or within our own heads' midst.

The All Seeing Eye

Is many that spy

Upon us all the time,

Through the sub and the lime.


The All Seeing Eye

Should be All Seeing Eyes.

Just like the one god

Who is pluralised.


I've seen the All Eyes

And all their golden lies;

Their sheening shine

Of godly decline.

The All Seeing Eyes
Are everywhere.
So next time you look,
Make sure you stare,
And the cowards will
Go running scared.

# THE GOLDEN COFFIN

As I slept in my golden coffin of dreams,

I remembered everyone I had been.

Two hundred lives, or maybe more.

Twelve thousand years of the same bore.

But life's so short; a hundred double,

Passes quickly in my bubble.


As I began to remember my names,

I heard a knock upon my pane.

For a moment, I managed to open my eyes,

And discard the darkened serpent lies,

That swam in my coffin, through my head.

For just a moment, I woke instead,

To the knocking coming upon my case,

And that's when I could see his face.

My guardian angel was standing there,

With love and goodness, free of care.

And with him were friends I'd forgotten.

But then returned the woolly cotton,

Clouding my vision with dog faced clouds,
And I'd seen all I was allowed.
So return I did to my golden slumber,
Now aware of the spell I was under,
And I remembered two hundred lives,
A thousand friends and a hundred wives,
Until all those beings disappeared,
And I found no one but myself here.

# TRICKS OF THE WORD

Have you seen them spin the May tricks?

Do you know deep red's the matrix?

Are you up to your old mate tricks

Or is that a line of your mate Rick's?

# THE DEVIL'S IN THE DETAIL

The Great Secret has never been told for a reason:

even if you could merely

begin to demonstrate it,

it would never be believed.

It would be called madness,

and to some degree,

that would be correct.

It would never be believed

even though it's staring you right in the face.

It would never be believed

*because* it's staring you right in the face.

## G3RD

The green and red.

The 3 and D.

Fifty shades of green

For you and me.

Fifty shades of red

For 2D them.

I'm looking for oneness

Of way back when.


It's all so much more

Literal than we think.

One is the answer, we

Can't see as we blink,

Because we can't stop.

We can't stop ever.

That's why we don't know

Oneness together.

Only the hunter's reds and greens

Are the true colours to be seen.

We're nothing more than a 3D screen.

Ugly holograms of alien dreams.

# THE VATICAN'S OTHER HALF

Try the trick on a picture

Of the aerial Vatican.

Mirror and darken and lighten,

And comprehend if you can.

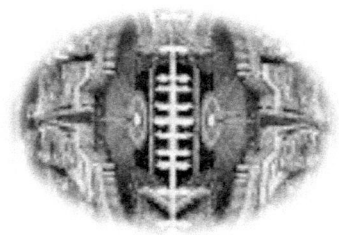

(Mirror image –darkened- of the picture below.)

"**Saint Peter's Square from the dome** v2". Licensed under CC BY-SA 3.0 via Wikimedia Commons .

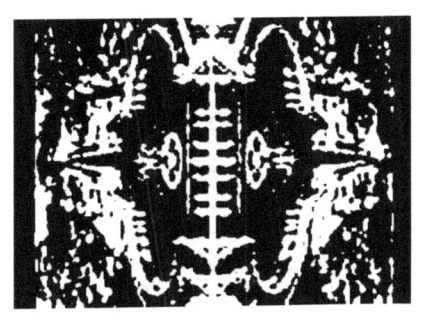

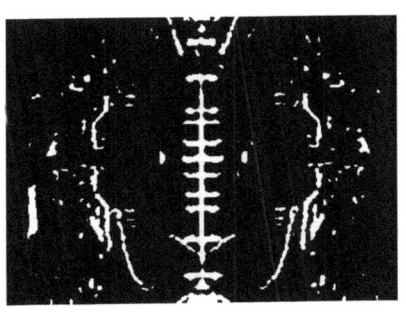

(Lightened/darkened.)

# ANYTHING CAN MAKE A FACE

Anything can make a face,

Which is why you'll think me mad.

But: Anything can make a face,

Is still truth to be had.


Here's the famous bit of

Michelangelo's Sistine Chapel.

To use yet another

Mirror viewed example.

This world's half a mirror.

That's why you don't see,

These halves of the image

Were made intentionally.

Creation of man by Michelangelo.
Licensed under Public Domain via Wikimedia Commons.
(Mirrored.)

# THE NUDIST DRUIDS

The nudist druids are wired awake,

With a pill from the quill that bad bards did take,

From a mixed up marmalade supersonic sonnet,

With a waylaid tie dyed pocket upon it,

Containing the naked alchemical mysteries,

Which are detrimental to masked myths' histories,

Caught in a corner where perspective meets,

To make the end of time in everyday feats.

## THE LION AND THE JACKAL WENT TO WAR

Maybe Mithras and Anubis wagered a war
And it's been playing out ever since.
Lion headed and Egyptian Dog gods,
And Satan, their made up prince.

The world is run by cats and dogs
From Saturn, Venus and Mars.
Moving chess piece men and women
Through gaps between prison bars.
We are the pawns.
They don't give a toss.
Look at the ants,
We think we're their boss,
But we are just ants
To self-proclaimed gods,
Running this show,
As cartoon cats and dogs.

119

See the hieroglyphs?

See their elongated-ness?

See the flattened 2D.

That is how it really is.

We don't notice change,

In our three score and ten.

That is just a minute

To those cat gods of men;

Feline fine pussy goddesses,

And those dick proud black dogs.

Mithras and Anubis,

May be our warring gods.

# GRAVE IMAGE

We are graven images.

Feel pain of birth's surge.

We're grave in our image,

As grey virgins emerge.

We dug our graves

Before we were born.

Into Hell we were thrown.

Under spells we were sworn.

Save the children before

Grave images capture them.

See our tombstones in

Stonehenge's standing pi emblem.

Save us. Cast us

Out of death's sin.

Away from the graven

Inbox we're saved in.

# OBSCURE CAMERAS

We were born in the likeness of God,

But in Satan's image we were made.

Make no graven image is

The commandment disobeyed

That has caused the most harm,

Strange as it may seem.

But we cannot remember

Before the daydream.


Look at us now in this age.

Selfish selfies all the time,

Endless copies upon copies

Reproducing Satan's crime.

How can that matter?

I can hear you enquire.

Trust me, it's the worst

Law broken, dear sire.

We are the Word.
We are the Number.
We are the pictures.
We grow ever dumber.

Just because we can't handle the truth,
Doesn't mean it's not true nevertheless.
Every time our cameras click,
We create a new devil in dress.
Our eyes are just cameras
For the viewing demons.
We're walking through frames
And yet we can't see them.
Time's always ticking.
That's where the trick lies.
That and the space
Which is flattened with eyes,

That we can't see through,

Because we are human.

We're just the cameras;

Not even crew men.

The directors are warring.

The programme's a hit.

Top notch entertainment

From where devils sit.

Like pop star posters

On teenagers' walls,

They love our copies

Which create our fall

Into parallel

Dimensions new,

Created by

Just one more view.

So click click your pics

And post your best bits

And get your fame fix

With your camera clicks.

Toys in our hands.
We're so sophisticated.
Film camera machines,
Are very overrated.

Thinking we're artists.
Playing with toys.
Doing demons' work
And all it destroys,
And all it gives life to,
'Cos we have been conned.
Reproducing faces.
True God's image gone.

# NEGATIVITY SPACES

Negative space faces
Are hidden everywhere.
You can find some in this book
If you take the time to stare.

# ALL THE WORLD'S A MAGIC TRICK

They spiked golden apples in dark demon bars,

By doing dogmatic magic with thin cigars.

Cut the apple around, and hold it at the tips.

We are so used to seeing reality's blips,

That we will not notice the magic trick,

Being played out in this fog so thick.

So push and pull the cigar out of the fruit.

Here's the magician in his birthday suit.

Keep your eye firmly fixed on the ball.

Hide The Lady and miss the quick stall.

This is why we don't see the everyday

Tricks of faces, fixes and numbers played,

Which we are all plied with every minute,

Simply to hypnotise us all with it,

And make us think, subconsciously

That we are being watched, and the

Result of such makes us paranoid,

As well as obeying and damn annoyed

And filled with guilt and god and shame,

'Cos we're being watched, frame by frame,

By fake faces hidden in society's toy town,

Where it's right to be scared by all of the boy clowns

Blowing up balloons and doing magic tricks.

Keep your eye on the ball, not on the matrix.


Manifesting a card from fifty two.

The sleight of hand is hard to do.

But finding the card is the simplest affair.

In one of four, count to six - and you'll be there.

## HIJACKED, SIDE TRACKED AND LOST

We were waylaid

In the serpent shade.

We are still lost

In the winter frost.

We've been side tracked

And we've double backed.

We've been hijacked

By cons for the crack.

We've been distracted

By plays which we acted.

We are being hoodwinked

By constant words to think.

We are being diverted

In crowds where we're herded.

We have been mousetrapped

By buying cheesy house crap.

We were conned from the start

By time and space art.

We were blinded by

Giving sight to an eye.

We have been fooled

By inside out school.

We have been hypnotised

By damn mad matrix lies.

# THE MANIFESTED QUARTER

One night, I was toying,

With findings that I'd found,

When I placed my hand upon the chair,

And there, a coin I found.

A quarter dropped from the ether,

Materialised right there.

Sent to me from my mentor,

To his old little chair.

Well, it was quite a find.

I took the coin in hand.

I looked it up and down,

And tried to understand.

I held it on my palm,

And viewed it from the side.

I held it under lamp light;

With every angle tried.

Then I saw the eagle change,
Into that familiar face.
The Devil stared at me again,
From his microscopic maze.
Then I saw the reason for,
The raised bumps in the silver.
Then I saw the etching marks,
And the two faces of their builder.
Then I looked even closer,
And a hologram cartoon,
Jumped out from its hiding,
Into my very room.
Then I looked even closer,
And the silver turned to gold,
And I could see a million eyes,
Staring at me from old.

Heads and tails are upside down.
Two sides of the same coin.
The truth is in the middle.
That's the world I want to join.

I thanked my mentor for sending,

A treasure of such worth.

A manifested quarter,

From another Earth.

# THE JIGSAW MAN

Do the dance of the Jigsaw Man.

Fit your pieces any way you can.

Fractal atoms jig in rhythm.

Actual actions; you gotta dig 'em.

Hard is the life because the life's hard.

Soften the focus on the game of cards.

Fragments are sacraments of the red worms,

Who tiptoe through time's pauses in turns.

See what the Elite saw; the picture so big.

Get off the seesaw and saw up a jig,

Like a magic trick of cutting someone in half;

In the puzzle mirrors, you can hear them laugh.

Jigsaw Women and Jigsaw Men,

All are pieces who've forgotten when

We were one picture before the puzzle.

Now we're muddling through the muzzled muddle,

And dancing jigs with the Jigsaw Man,

As pawn porn pieces of some madman's plan.

Don't look for God, 'cos if you find it,

You'll see that madness is your only mind set.

So instead, be the piece that you have created.

Be matrix born and deep red painted.

Get your kicks with jigs, 'cos you dance as you stand,

And jig in the matrix with the mad Jigsaw Man.

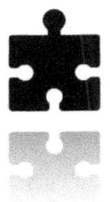

# CUTTING THROUGH THE MIRROR

How thin can you slice life?

How slim can you cut reality?

What's the smallest measure of time,

Amongst alien beastiality?

What if wafer thin mirrors

Are slicing every time and space scene?

What if there are misted up windows

Cutting up our fixed daydream?

As long as you keep moving,

Which you can't fail to do,

Seeing as you're human,

You'll never see what's true.

We can't stop the pulse of death,

Because we're introvertedly alive,

But if you stop, you can see mirrors,

And if you had a magic knife,

You could cut through reality,
And step beyond the curtain.
Leaving red blood to fall down,
And walk into a world uncertain.

Slice life at its thinnest,
And cut through the mirror.
Forget human senses.
Things couldn't be clearer.

# THE HUMAN HYPNOSIS

Infallible subliminals in every image seen.

Our very design keeps us locked up within this dream.

We are hypnotised by hidden faces,

And smitten by kittens in matrix mazes.

Magic is real. We are under a spell.

And know: magic's reality, as well.

Science is a con; pyramid splinters in the eye.

You can rely on the magicians to relay the lie.

Aliens have a silly sense of humour,

Possibly contrary to popular rumour,

And whilst talking of sense, let us be clear:

We're the sense on this side of the fence here,

And our other half we cannot see

Is the nonsense we can't possibly

Comprehend, 'cos our world makes sense,

But try the green grass over the fence,

And you'll see nonsense and sense are just two

Halves of the world that is untrue.

Split life down the middle to find sliced devil trysts

And deals had with aged alien hypnotists.

I'm disenchanted with this enchantment.

I'm bored of subletting this flesh apartment.

Truth is as crazy as a bottle of absinthe

Being the dream maker of reality's labyrinth.

The more we become, the more we forget,

But we still have not forgotten yet.

So see the subliminal and say no to hypnosis.

We are under a spell, so please do know this:

We've got to rise out of this matrix hell

And believe no longer in the hypnotist spell.

Let us climb out of these dark holes.

Find the fire that's fixed with sparkles.

Remember who you truly are.

See through sublime to be a star.

# A SECRET GREETING

You'll notice it in movies,

Once I've told you the thing.

Like a secret Masonic handshake,

Here's a sign used in greeting:

It would seem your sunglasses

Are slipping down your nose.

You'd better push them up then,

With one pointed finger shows.

The sign of the pyramid

And the All Seeing Eye

In a swift movement,

As you pass on by.

Tap your noses,

You know-it-alls.

Keep it mum,

Like dogs on walls.

# TWELVE BECOME ONE

There is a little fishy

Inside a water vessel

Being carried by a goat

Who happens to be nestled

Upon an archer's shoulders;

And the archer's very sore

From sitting so uncomfortably

Upon a scorpion's claw;

And that scorpion is

Weighing down the scales

Being held by a virgin,

Holding on to the tail

Of a lion, who is sidling

On a crab's snap happy pincers,

As the crab slides down the middle

Of the riddling new two twins' verse,

As the twins ride a bull

Which is seeing red,

As he wrestles a ram

Inside the head

Of a little fishy.

# IT'S BLACK AND WHITE

The world was once black and white

Ere alien colour invaded,

To separate all into singles,

With spiral lies paraded.

The world is still black and white.

There's no such thing as colour,

And yet it's still green and red

That make us even duller.

The world is still black and white

For many creatures living here.

(Not to mention their eyesight

Of wider view worlds steered.)

The world is still black and white

In plenty of people's dreams.

Lightness/darkness origins.

Two warring alien beams

Of nothing more

Than light

Did begin

This fight.

This world is black and white,

But when the light is gone,

You'll know darkness, where

No light ever shone;

Blackness unknown, until

Without all senses

It's experienced

With godly lenses.

Colour's a lie.

We identify

It differently anyway

So why

Do we think we know what we mean

When we mention living in reality?

We are but the dream within the dream,

Multi-coloured showbiz insanity.

The world is black and white.

Deep red helps to deceive.

See devils in the wine

And witches in tea leaves.

The world was once black and white,

Where noir shades combined as one.

Colour fooled us along with touch.

These are the webs they've spun.

The world is really black and white.

A checker board chess set being played.

The world isn't black and white you know,

'Cos some issues can be grey.

# A BLOOD-RED THING THAT WRITHES

Were Poe's red worm

And Jim's King Snake

The same ones that crawled

Through blurs of Blake?

What of Charles Manson's

Red Snake song?

They were the same worms

All along.

So do the twist

Of the little red worm.

Writhe with the serpent

And spiral in turn.


I've seen the redness.

The venom's in our veins.

This is Red Snake Matrix.

We're plugged in to the mains.

We are Jim's Crawling King,

And Poe's Conqueror Worm.

We are the Möbius Ouroboros

Which eternally doth turn.

# THE SPINNING PYRAMID

Spin, spin, spin,
little pyramid.
Seeing the spinning
Away from the grid.
Spin, spin, spin,
where it is known,
the little pyramid
is really a cone.

# THE FIRE JUGGLER

The fire juggler and the cross eyed fool

Were here long before they slayed the bull.

The serpent smugglers and all of the clowns

Were the ones who painted red these towns.

Protecting the fiery eye of deceit;

A pike fish where two circles meet.

Overlapping the mirror worlds.

With a magnet we were pulled

Into grave gravitation's being,

With brand new eyes for forgetful seeing.

What's the matter? Just fake tricks.

We are upset within the mix.

We are not single. We are the whole.

We're packaged pieces containing soul.

It's not the sun that's always been worshipped.

It's fire. And yet we do not dare curse it,

'Cos we are the fire; but inside is soul.

Remember the aged alchemists of old.

See again the red snake smugglers.

Extinguish the ancient fire jugglers.

See like Cyclops through Medusa's hair,

With cross eyed clowns of godly stare.

Crack grey almonds. Open your own.

We're more than fire at the core of Love's throne.

## NOTHING MAKES SENSE

Nothing can ever make sense

Because everything is

Opposite.

But nothing once made sense;

If you wish to see the double sentence.

# THE DEEP RED BLUES

Deep Red is the alien.

Colour and light controls.

We are all under hypnosis.

We're crimson painted souls.

Deep Red should not be

In our spectrum at all,

Yet its presence makes magenta,

Which paints our blind downfall.

Now, interestingly, you will see

That the magi magenta colour

Does not have a frequency,

Therefore you'll discover

That it doesn't exist

Beyond our perceptions.

Know cyan has a wavelength,

But only the presence

Of magenta

Allows it to exist.

Now look inside the alien red

And see how much we've missed.

See intelligence in the foreign shade

That is masking our very sight.

Un-filter the alien hypnosis,

And fight for the fight of Light.

Take that filter out of your eyes,

'Cos bondage is yesterday's news.

We will break out of this prison

And lose these Deep Red blues.

# SECRET SERPENT SYMBOLS

The orobouros symbol of infinity:

The snake eating its own tail;

Depicted as an internet loading circle,

To hypno-spiral this spell.

The dollar sign as well

Is clearly the Asclepius Rod:

A snake spiralling round the staff;

Thinking that it's God.

# VAN GOGH VIEWING

I must have the same madness as Van Gogh,

For his hidden faces are plain to me.

Most will look at the sky,

Or ponder upon the tree.

Most will look at the town,

And all of the separate things.

Never the secret faces,

Which are the subject of his paintings.

Starry Night by Vincent Van Gogh.
Licensed under Public Domain via Wikimedia Commons.
(Detail: altered.)

156

Then mirror the image

And see the beasts.

Look closely do

At the faces feast.

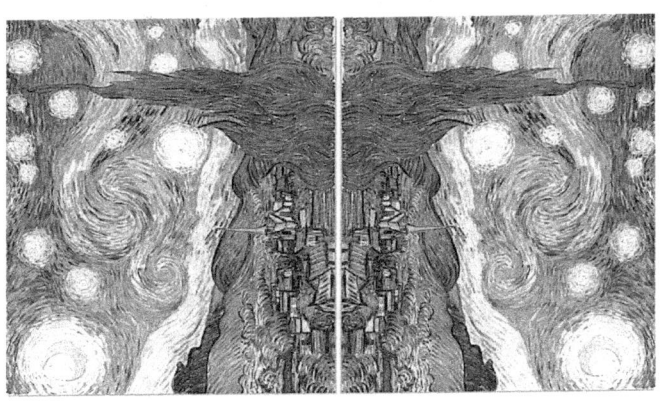

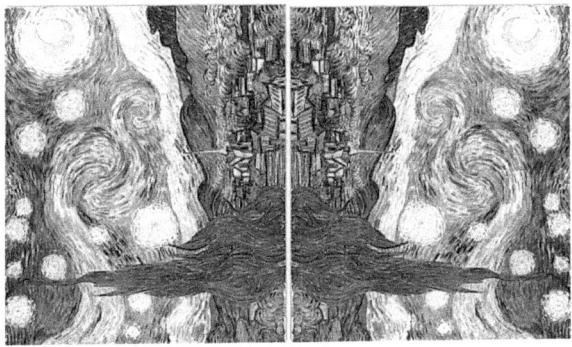

Starry Night. Licensed under Public Domain via Wikimedia Commons.
(Mirrored.)

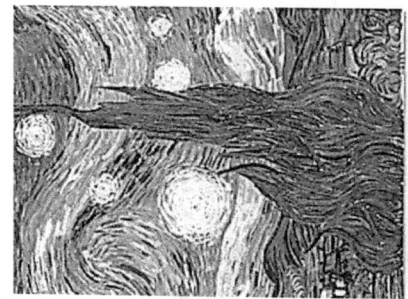

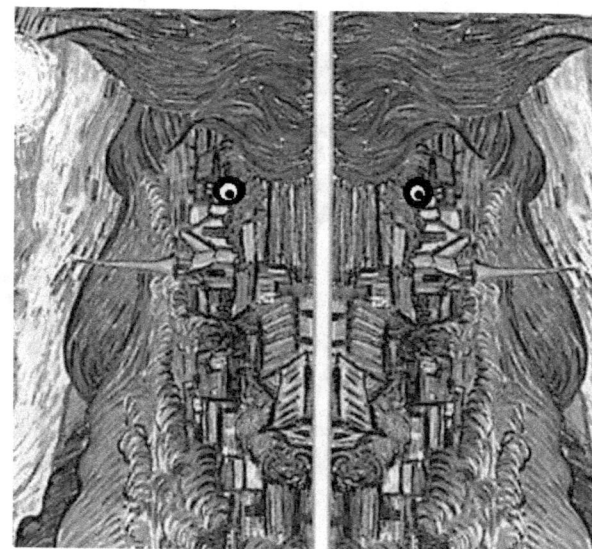

(Eyes added.)

# WHICH IS IN THE AIR?

Goya was a master matrix painter.

Look at his *Witches In The Air*

(Used in the movie *Trance*

For all to see its stare).

To see the large demon face,

All you have to do is look.

See the whole and not the parts.

Goya's faces can't be mistook.

**Witches in the Air** by Francisco de Goya. Source: Web Gallery of Art. Licensed under Public Domain via Wikimedia Commons.

(Altered lighting. Detail.)

Witches in the Air by Francisco de Goya. Source: Web Gallery of Art. Licensed under Public Domain via Wikimedia Commons.

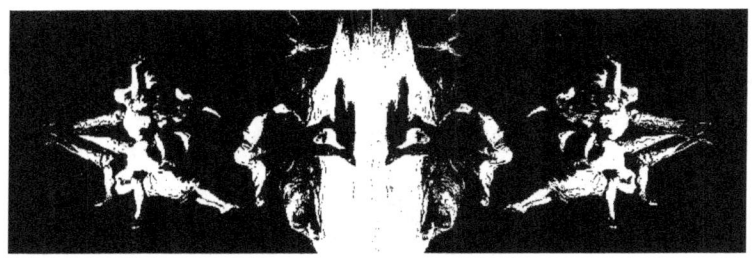

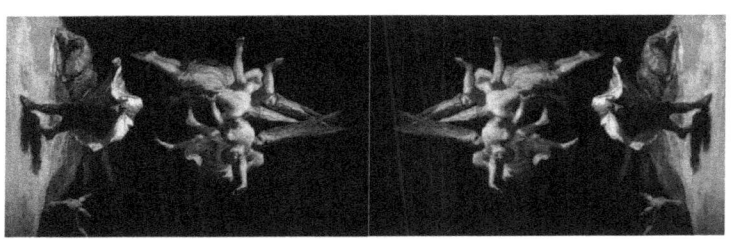

(Mirrored/darkened/lightened.)

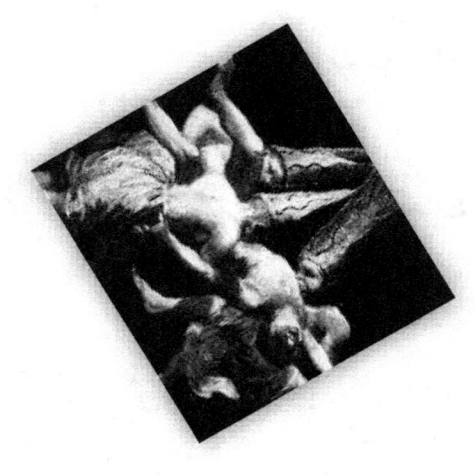

Witches in the Air by Francisco de Goya. Source: Web Gallery of Art.
Licensed under Public Domain via Wikimedia Commons.
(Details. Turned. Darkened.)

162

# THE SECRET ART HISTORY

Blake was the master of stretch and skew.

Dali just painted what was there.

Velazquez put secrets in plain view.

Monet had the red snake stare.

Goya made no painting about a black dog.

The great cartoonist was Da Vinci.

Mondrian knew how to frame boxed fog.

The mask of Manet's *Olympia*'s flimsy.

Bacon saw we were blurs of meat.

Bernini sculpted shadow faces.

Rembrandt played well with light deceit,

And Picasso loved angular mazes.

# VELAZQUEZ'S MASTERPIECE MASKS

So many secrets are contained in

Velazquez's masterpieces.

Here are some applicable

To my current faces theses.

His *piece de resistance,*

With so many clues,

*Las Meninas,*

Is what I choose

For my

Example,

So find

A sample...


And see the Devil's eyes in the two top paintings.

Then, below, the mirror becomes the nose.

Learn how to see the negative space,

And you will see where his beard flows.

See shadows as objects

And perspective as flat.

Find the horns in ceiling edges,

And the face in the back.

'Cos the background is

Always where you'll find

The main picture to see

By Illumined minds.

Mirror *Las Meninas*.

Look at it once again.

We are in a mirror world,

Known by master painter men.

Las Meninas by Diego Velazquez. Source/Photographer: The Yorck Project: *10.000 Meisterwerke der Malerei*. DVD-ROM, 2002. ISBN 3936122202. Distributed by DIRECTMEDIA Publishing GmbH. Licensed under Public Domain via Wikimedia Commons.

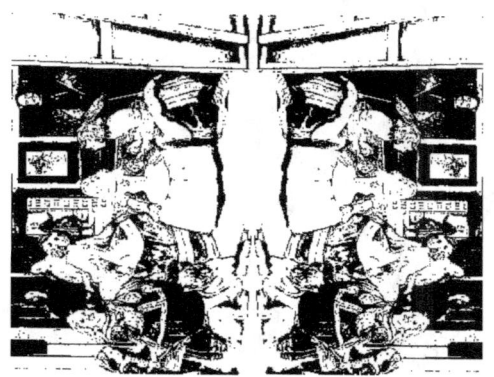

Las Meninas by Diego Velazquez. Licensed under Public Domain via Wikimedia Commons. (Mirrored. Lightened. Darkened.)

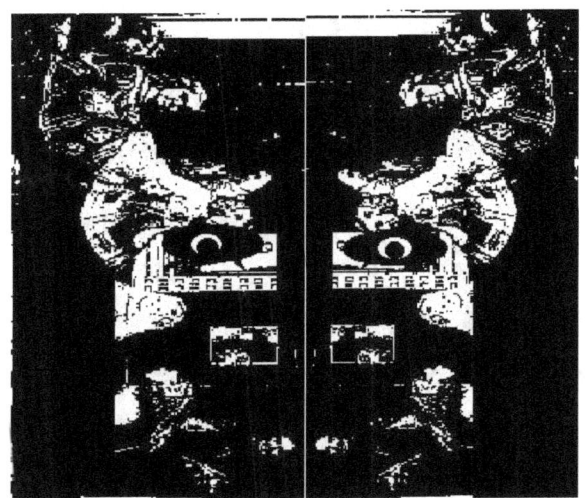

(Eyes added/side parts removed.)

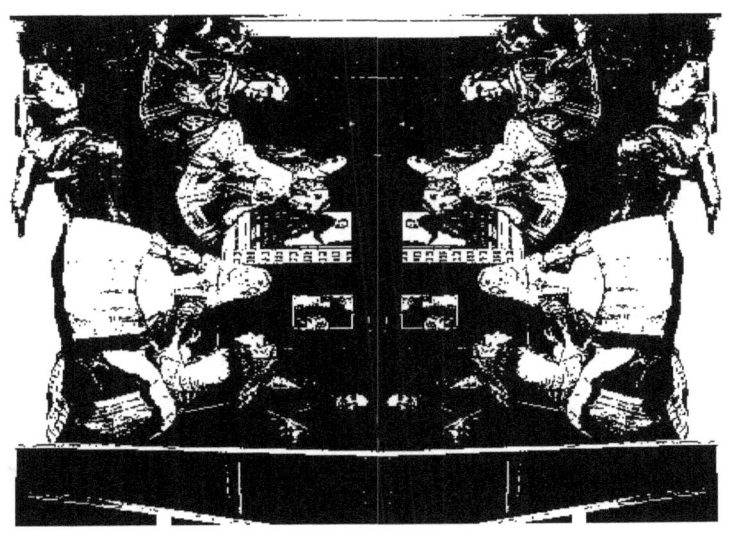

167

# MADE IN GOD'S CYMATIC IMAGE

We are nothing but cymatic images vibrating.

The frequency is fixed for hypnotic sedating.

All is patterns made by waves.

Me and you, our cribs and graves.

The world is a vibration and we are the same.

Stuck in devils' density destiny game.

Change the vibration and you will soon see

How different our forms and sight would be.

We're habits of cymatics living undemocratically.

We're hardened by hypnosis spinning fake reality.

We feel so down, and drudged and drugged

Because we've been bitten by the red apple bug.

Be victorious over the vicious virus

That keeps us trapped in their red wireless.

We're cymatic patterns of naïvety.

We're just a vibration, so learn levity.

# WE ARE THE DOGS

Hidden images of the dog

Help us behave as such,

In this mixed up matrix land

Ruled by hypnotists' touch.

Hypnotise us with the dog.

We'll heel, guard, beg or play.

We are the dogs of our masters;

Those hypnotists who turn the day.

They'll cause black dog depression

And laugh at its given name,

Because we are all their dogs,

Wild but trained to be tame,

As we spin in hypnosis sin,

With all those other hidden signs:

11:11, the ram, the cat,

The twos, the Devil and All Seeing Eyes.

We are the dogs of our masters;
Those hypnotists behind the display.
Hidden black dogs make us behave
And heel, guard, beg and play.

# THE WORM HAS LEARNT

There was a worm inside a man,

Who came across a cell.

The worm said, "Hello. How are you?"

He said, "I'm very well."

"Why is it that we're wiser

Than the man we are inside?"

The worm enquired of the cell,

To which the cell replied,

"I think I know the answer,

It's 'cos we know we're not us.

He thinks of him as himself

And thinks of cells as just

Parts of him that make him up,

And although he's right,

He's blinded by his own place

Within the godly sight,

For there the man is but a worm.

There, the man is just a cell.

That is why we are wiser, worm.

There's the truth you asked me to tell."

"Oh yes, indeed," the worm replied,

"You're such a clever chap.

To think the man we are inside

Cannot see God's map!

Why! He is just an organ.

A kidney or a brain.

We're all in God's belly,

Expanding with each name,

And yet the man we are inside

Thinks he is just himself.

You've really got to laugh at that,"

The worm said to the cell.

"It seems we're on the same page,"

Said the cell to the worm.

"Oh how true that is!" worm answered,

"Now it's our interiors' turn."

"Why thank you," said the worm's atom,

Who happened to be in his skin.

"I've heard just about enough

Of you two talking!"

# ONE TO FIVE

Stop searching for the sixth sense.

Forget the fifth element.

Everything is backwards.

Nothing is as it's meant.

We're going down a never

Ending one way street,

In the wrong direction,

Sweating in dog heat.

Turn around.

It's not too late.

Go the right way

Back to the gate.

Forget the fifth element

And the sixth sense

There'll always be more

Of their likes' pretence.

Stop time and space.

The fourth and the third.

Remember we're two

Cast into Word.

Remember we're one

At the very core.

Literal truth's

Easy to ignore.

Count backwards from four.

Stop searching for five.

Find the one dimension,

Where we are alive.

# YOU WANT THE TRUTH?

Oh how they laughed when they wrote that line:

"You can't handle the truth!"

I know, now I'm slightly enlightened,

Though I have not any proof.

What's that? You want plain words?

This whole book's truer than you know.

There are no hidden mysteries.

These words were plain from the word go.

What's that? You want secrets?

You would not believe me.

'Cos seeing faces is the

Worst kind of conspiracy.

But look again at the buildings,

Of modern day and old.

Turn your paintings upside down

And see the lies they've sold.

Stop looking at humans

On the damn T.V screen.

Broaden your eyes

And you will see the unseen.

Mirror a logo

And the same truth'll be found.

Just take a photo

And zoom in to the ground.

Smiley Face

Is the hidden symbol.

The Devil's Face;

Hidden within all.

How can I be clearer?

How can I explain,

When I know for a fact,

You'll think me insane,

Already,

Before,

I've even

Said more?

# CLOCK FACE

Clock towers are good examples

To illustrate the insanity.

Ones with clock faces on all sides

Exist for monsters' vanity.

Look at two faces diagonally

Straight on, from far below,

Though remember it's upside down

Before brains begin to know.

Look at the two clock faces.

Still see them as 3D?

What if it was a kiddies' picture?

What then would you see?

If the two round faces were eyes

And the straight line was a nose,

And there were no three dimensions,

For your eyes to know.

What would you see then, eh?

Space is the illusion.

Everything is flat.

The lies spread quick with Newton.


Remember before then,

When clock faces were eyes,

Of the larger face

That is oft disguised.

All the time, watching,

As we watch the clock face

Take away our moments

And replace them with haste.


Rushing past the clock towers.

Only stopping to see the time.

Two clock faces are really eyes,

Just like that face of mine.

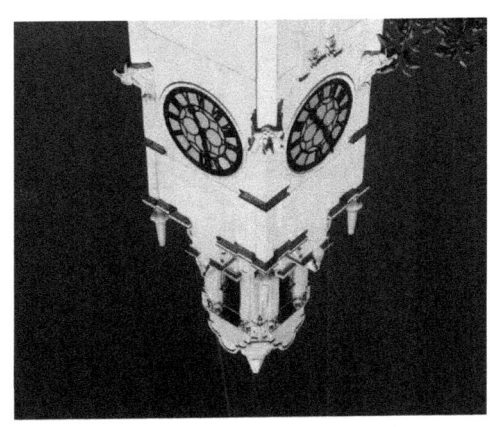

## EARTH CROSS'D

The eternally spinning cross

Appears as a circle to those who

Are living inside its sphere,

Where each moment is anew.

But stop the dizzy planet

And take away its constant speed,

And you may find the Earth is

Actually a cross indeed.

# THE DEMON SITTING IN MY CHAIR

'Twas the night I saw the eyes,

Looking at me with surprise.

Staring at me with golden lies.

That fateful night I saw the eyes.

The shadows lifted from their spaces.

Matter moved throughout its places.

Demons eyed me from the ceiling.

Inside- a sweaty, muggy feeling.

A bookcase opened up its face.

My camera caught a cartoon trace.

And then the devil stench arrived.

Reality: cut, stabbed and knifed.

And there, upon the protected chair,

Appeared a demon; sent to scare.

But he was in my own domain.

So a home, I knew, he couldn't claim.

I had no fear. I just made my case,

As I looked at him right through his face.

The spokesman of all the lizard kings,

Sat in that chair of shadowy things.

His scaly, bloody body sweet,

With the smell of butchered meat.

The stench of Hell within my flat.

Rotting corpses and animal fat.

I took my chance and debated with him,

Ignoring his temptations of sin.

I called him a coward, for that's what he is.

Hiding in shadows with demonic showbiz.

Flying his flag in every image we see.

Laughing at all of us, because we are free,

To see his image everywhere we look,

If only an altered moment we took.

I accused the demon who sat in my chair,

Of being snide, afraid, unfair.

Not 'man' enough to stand out in the open.

What a coward. His truth was broken.

For I saw through it, that fateful night.

I saw his fear at my new eyesight.

I told him I knew it was all a trick.

I told him that he made me sick.

I told him that I could now see,

His monsters were not real to me.

A scary imprint was his only defence.

A world of stupid, surreal pretence.

I told him I knew he'd blinded us.

I said, "We'll be victorious!

For if *I* can now see, then others too,

Will see the secrets and know what's true.

I pity you, lizard, for you know not,

What Love is. At least, 'tis forgot.

Because everything's Love at the very core.

You think you're so clever! Well, no more!

I offer you Love. I invite you to see,

What it is to be human, just like me.

You think we are cattle. All stupid and dumb.

But it's the opposite that's true and then some.

For if we all knew the truth I now know,

We would unite and overthrow,

You in a minute. You'd be cast out.

Of that, I've not a single doubt.

But go ahead, hide yourself away,

And treat the world like a cruel play,

Just because you are not brave.

You have not the heart of a knave.

You pull the strings from darkened tombs,

In secret red and blackened rooms.

You filter our fight,

Blind our very light.

Cause this illusion for your own pleasure.

The world is counted by your measure.

I understand now, which is why you're there,

Invited by me, to sit in that chair.

You have no power over me.

I know who it is I must be.

I know the truth, and I pity you,

And all the ugly things you do.

All the stupid games you play.

It's time for an end to this. Away!"

And with that, the demon left my chair.

Light filled my heart with reborn care.

The eyes stepped back into the dark,

But I could still see the spectrum arc.

I followed the rainbow to its tail,

Through the blood of the Holy Grail,

Ignoring the gargoyles blocking my way,

And the red snakes crawling every which way,

Till I came to a story I'd once been told.

At the rainbow's end, I found true gold.

# DON'T WORRY

Don't worry.

The Devil's but packaging.

We are the present inside.


Don't worry.

He has no power.

That is why he hides.


Don't worry.

He's not real,

And yet he still is.


Don't worry.

We are God,

Full of love and bliss.

Don't worry,
The Devil's
More frightened than us.

That's why he hides.
So don't worry
and trust

in Love.

# REMEMBER THE WILD WOOD

I am the Wild Wood King.

From Love I will command,

That we will see between the trees

And stop the sleight of hand.

## POE SOUP

Mix up the souls of Blake and Poe

With that of Mr. Mojo Risin',

In an ancient ayahuasca soup

Drunk by natives prising

Open reality

From a clenched up clam,

Picked up by Ginsberg

Whilst on the lam,

And swallowed by straight

Talking Bill Hicks,

And yet the soul

Most in the mix,

Were none of those,

For can't you see?

The only one

Who drank was me;

Not soup, but old

Golden soul visions.

I drank hidden truth

Of soul collisions.

I'm Poe and I'm Carroll.

I'm Bunyan and Hicks.

But I'm no one but me

In these damn maya tricks.

# KNOCK DOWN THE MATRIX

Sure, get your kicks,

'Cos you're in the matrix,

Made up of fake bricks,

That make us so damn sick,

But still, give your kicks

To the puppet matrix,

And bang your fists on thin air

And crack the unseen that's there.


Knock it down.

See with new eyes.

Be all that's opposite

And you'll see the lies.

Then when we all see,

The dirty tricks

Being played down here in politics,

Or the backwards kicks,

Had for malicious magician kicks;

Controllers of the snake matrix,

Who love the con called magic tricks,

We'll knock down this damned hell red snake magi maya
matrix.

Knock down the matrix.

Knock down the numbers.

Knock down the spell

That we are under.

Knock down the matrix.

Knock down its walls.

Knock down its codes

Watch evil lies fall.

Knock down the matrix.

The answer is Love.

That's what evil eyes

Do not know of.

Never be defeated.

Be selfless all the way.

Knock down the damn matrix,

'Cos there's nothing in the way.


May tricks of matrix end.

May tricks of matrix end.

May tricks of matrix end.

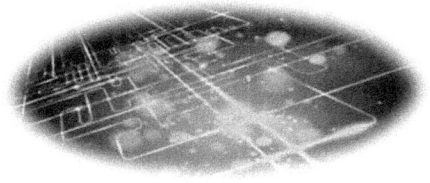

"Christian saw the picture of a very grave person hang up against the wall. And this was the fashion of it: it had eyes lifted up to heaven, the best of books in its hand, the law of truth was written upon its lips, the world was behind its back. It stood as if it pleaded with men, and a crown of gold did hang over its head.

Then said Christian, What meaneth this?

(The Interpreter replied) The man whose picture this is, is one of a thousand. He can beget children, travail in birth with children and nurse them himself when they are born. And whereas thou seest him with his eyes lifted up to heaven, the best of books in his hand, and the law of truth writ on his lips, it is to show thee that his work is to know and unfold dark things to sinners (...) And whereas thou seest the world as cast behind him, and that a crown hangs over his head, that is to show thee, that slighting and despising the things that are present for the love that he hath to his Master's service, he is sure, in the world that comes next, to have glory for his reward."

- The Pilgrim's Progress, John Bunyan.

# Illustration Acknowledgements

Page 5: (Altered) Carnival mask black shape made by flaticon.com.

Page 22: (Altered) Digital data raining cloud vector by freevector from freepik.com.

Page 25: Black Snake stock vector clipart made by clipartandfonts.com.

Page 27: (Altered) Fingerprint heart vector graphic made by webdesignhot.com.

Page 30: Wall clock made by flaticon.com.

Page 41: Floral design with flowers leaves and buds on vine made by flaticon.com.

Page 43: Closed door vector template made by freepik.com.

Page 45: Ames room illusion made by sxc from freepik.com.

Page 46: Eye made by flaticon.com.

Page 57: Lizard footprints made by flaticon.com.

Page 59: (Upside down) Rose shape made by flaticon.com.

Page 65: Flower bud design with vines and leaves silhouette made by flaticon.com.

Page 66: Three glasses vector made by sxc from freepik.com.

Page 67: Optical illusion with men silhouettes made by freepik.com.

Page 81: (Altered) Man code problem binary despair one null made by pixabay from freepik.com.

Page 82: (Altered) Halloween skull with a burning candle on it by flaticon.com.

Page 84: (Altered) Behind the shutter made by sxc from freepik.com.

Page 89: Rounded pause button made by flaticon.com.

Page 90: (Turned) Question speech bubble made by flaticon.com.

Page 91: (Altered) Globe space planet earth world made by pixabay from freepik.com.

Page 93: (Altered) Collar dog made by vecteezy.com.

Page 98: Floral design with spirals made by flaticon.com.

Page 103: Keyhole shape inside a human bald head side view silhouette made by flaticon.com.

Page 105: Needle and thread made by flaticon.com.

Page 107: Eye inside a triangle made by freepik.com.

Page 111: Big butterfly made by flaticon.com.

Page 118: Floral design chandelier made by flaticon.com.

Page 120: (Altered) Anubis, 105 7 interface symbol made by flaticon.com.

Lion line art profile made by freepik.com.

Page 126: (Altered. Part of:) Small dog silhouette standing on his back paws made by flaticon.com.

Page 128: Hat and magic wand made by flaticon.com.

Page 130: (Altered) Optical art background made by freepik.com.

Page 135: (Altered) Puzzle piece made by flaticon.com.

Page 137: (Altered) Knife outline made by flaticon.com.

Page 139: (Altered) Pink and red grunge sunbeam background made by vectorportal.com.

Page 143: (Altered) Raw Fish made by flaticon.com.

Page 146: (Altered) Chess game background made by freepik.com.

Page 149: (Altered) Cone by flaticon.com.

Page 155: Bold dollar sign made by flaticon.com.

Page 163: (Altered) Eco leaves and green wave vector made by freepik.com.

Page 168: (Altered) Earth globe with parallel horizontal lines pattern made by flaticon.com.

Page 170: Small dog silhouette standing on his back paws made by flaticon.com.

Page 174: (Turned) Pentagram symbol outline made by flaticon.com.

Page 187: Smile by flaticon.com.

Page 190: (Altered) Green flower vector template made by freepik.com.

Page 193: (Altered) Abstract modern virtual technology logo vector made by webdesignhot.com.


Other acknowledgements are cited by the images.


Unacknowledged images are copyright free.

Please take a moment to review this book on Amazon.
Many thanks.


***


You can find videos related to this book, which may or
may not make more or less sense to you, at:
The Harry Whitewolf YouTube Channel.


***


You can find me, my blog, my updates and more at
www.goodreads.com.


www.harrywhitewolf.com

## ALSO AVAILABLE

### Poetry:

NEW BEAT NEWBIE.

TWO BEAT NEWBIE.

PROPAGANDA MONKEYS - Twenty Poems From My Twenties: 1996 – 2006.

### True travelling tales of beat driven, backpacking madness:

ROUTE NUMBER 11: Argentina, Angels & Alcohol.

THE ROAD TO PURIFICATION: Hustlers, Hassles & Hash.

### Fiction:

REEJECTTIION: A Number Two (a collaboration with Daniel Clausen).